Lightning Forest, Lava Root

Lightning Forest, Lava Root

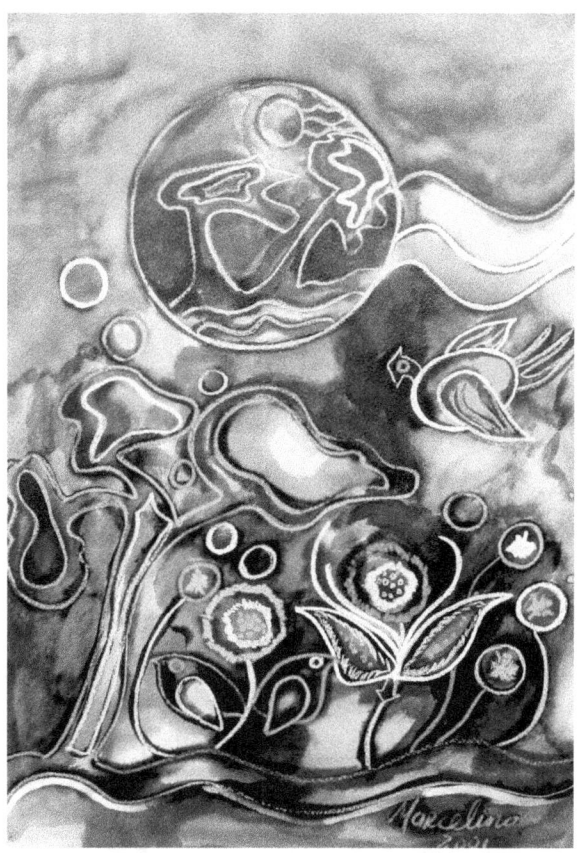

Erica Maria Litz

Plain View Press
P. O. 42255
Austin, TX 78704

plainviewpress.net
sb@plainviewpress.net
1-512-441-2452

Copyright Erica Maria Litz 2009. All rights reserved.
ISBN: 978-0-9819731-5-9
Library of Congress Number: 2009928091

Cover art by Marcelino González
    http://pwp.etb.net.co/marcelinogp/index.html
Cover design by Susan Bright

Acknowledgements

Gratitude goes to the following publications for first printing these poems: "Namesake" and "La Despierta" in *The Caribbean Writer*, Vol. 19, 2005; "Come together, all of you—sobrinos, children—and listen:" 1st appeared in *quietShorts*, Vol. 1, Issue 2, 2006; "Come together, all of you—sobrinos, children—and listen:" later appeared in *Americanisado*, 2008; "Gracia's Walk" and "One hand on a hip preferring" in *Superstition Review*, v.1,n1, 2008; "Birthright," "Té de Limón," and "Agua Panela" in *Superstition Review*, v.1, n.2, 2008; "Tia's Request" in *Moondance*, January 2009; "Twelve Poems for Mama, Her Hands, and Fire They Started" in *Oranges & Sardines*, Issue 3, Winter 2008; "First Dance" in *Brink Magazine*, October 2008; "Numina" in *Literary Mama*, November 2008; "The Sugar Beet Prayer," and "You Fear Thunder and Ants" in *HCR 2009 Edition*..

Dedicated to

Iria and Joseph

Contents

I.

You Fear Thunder and Ants	13
Come together, all of you—*sobrinos*, children—and listen:	14
The First Dance	26
Adolescent American	27
Periluna	28
El Motivo	29
Grab a Stick	30
When Magdalena Descended	31
Wet Claw, Half-Eaten	32
Arracatacataca	33
Agua Panela	34

II.

Birthright	39
La Despierta	40
La Costa	41
Té de Límon	42
Look Longer	43
Menta Negra	44
The Queen of Colombia	45
Gracia's Walk	46
Namesake	47
Her Resurrection	48
One hand on a hip, preferring	49
Numina	50
Chispa en la Barriga de Dios	51
La Virgen de Chinquinquirá	52

III.

A Killing in the State of Cauca	55
The Sugar Beet Prayer	56
Refining Sugar	57
Peace Negotiations	58
Terremoto	59

Cáscara de Coco	60
The Suicide of El Dorado's Wife	61
Tia's Request	62
Ars Poetica	63
Twelve Poems for Mama, Her Hands, and the Fire They Started	64
Eduardo in June	76
About the Author	77

"The volcano's children flow down,
flow down the sides like lava
with their bouquets of flowers,
meandering down like roots,
like rivers."

"Bajan los niños del volcán,
bajan como la lava
con sus ramos de flores
como raíces bajan,
como ríos."

~Claribel Alegría from *Flores del volcán*

I.

You Fear Thunder and Ants

Daughter, we come from the cloud forests
Of the Andes and maybe you have
Some ancestral memory of running
Up a lost trail to hide
And not get washed away
By the politics of an ancient invasion

I've heard that the ants that nip
At your heels are fire ants
Whose ancestors originated from South America
And made their way to our northern desert garden

The year before you were conceived, I walked
Out the backdoor to see two Amazons perched on the back fence
Just after a desert morning monsoon rain

Or maybe you just don't like the so loud and hot pain
Of being small in a storm

Come together, all of you—*sobrinos*, children—and listen:

I.

Wanting to know the Andes—my grandfather's knees,
the Magdalena River—my grandmother's dirty dishwater,
I pined for a certain cornmeal,
a sampling in my pocket, the dust I rub between two meats,
my thumb and fingers.

To return to the place I first tasted,   I don't fly,
   I dive.   Beneath each country, I run
  into dirt. Head first,   my nose into bones,
   I dig with my teeth, burrow   carved stones, and roots,
tunnels under the southern borders,   tunnels caved-in by
clods of earth, skulls...

  But the borders aren't lines   I drag by my sides,
   they're all of Mexico, Central America,   my fingers caught in
the eye-holes
   beyond Panama and its canal.   I choke and cough blood,
     the faults open, and erupt.   Blood flows. The lava,
the burning-remains of pain   scourge-out a new through-way,
     one that blisters my feet again,   but being above ground
            I can run for the river.

II.

Back home in a garden of sweet acacia and cracked clay,
my lover waits for me,
patient for what will become cinnamon
and plankton, our children,
patient for my body,
and Chimizapagua, the Messenger who gave us
our ceremony: *Gold Rings by the Side of the Sink*.
The instructions: "Fill an enameled bowl at Tequendama,
                the great waterfall. Pinch cornmeal,
                dust it over the water, fade
                the stenciled rose into a fury of white.
                Tighten the fingers together to mix, add
                and add slowly. To be free of lumps,
                close your eyes.

                Knead several balls of dough.
                Hold the bowl close, because Chibchacum shifts
                the world from shoulder to shoulder.
                When he's careless, he moves
                the earth under your feet.

                Take each *bola* into hand,
                press life-lines into love-lines. Push
                palms in accordion motions,
                patting to flatten,
                turning to compress the edges.

                Blow a panpipe,
                because each note stokes the fire.
                Then place each *arepa* on the *parrilla*.

continued...

Cook them until they're charred,
cracked, and yellow,
like the black and gold gorges
writhed souls pass through.
Listen, lift them with fingernails.
Do add salt, and with each,
drink coffee,
guanabana juice,
or milk.

When you're full,
close your eyes halfway,
crossing the river between your minds
in a boat made with the webs of spiders."

III.

Zué, my Uncle Fire, met me on the bank.
His burning carried smoke to the coast,
carried smoke to the fanged, stone statues
squatting and anchoring against tremors of earth.

This uncle gave me a smoldering banana leaf
to ward off fighting dogs,
an accordion to keep my feet moving,
spells of feral rain,
and vizcacha fur for my navel
when I find it.

Knowing she'd teach me to float on mud
for Luis Fernando, I followed the Magdalena.
I told my uncle: *I'll face the crowds of the Left, the Right. For my cousin,*
I'll draw them in with my hand dropping
so the fingers snap,
like when I've touched something hot.
I'll say: My cousin is dead.
There are causes
(civil war, etc...),
but children learn—
Never let it end
without a fight.

Walking between the rows of polarized men,
I'll turn my wrist downside up,
drop my palm and pray—Tails—
until one grows from their coccyges.

continued...

*Hideous, but at least they'd be looking
to their own back, seeing
the other's forward,
when they were brothers
who talked over coffee through the night,
who talked until the matter was understood,
until giving gave without a hoarding or a holler,
until neighbors built—no hand better,
no help, worse—
just a place to raise a roof,
and dance.*

IV.

Tired of following, I whistled a cumbia,
squawked—¡*Maizal!*—flew over the Rio Cauca.
My hair, what was left of feathers,
what was left of a time when the breath of blackbirds
incited life, excited mountains to green.
My hair, contrails in the Andean sky, recalls Iraca, the Moon Chía,
who dropped her saliva in my ovaries
so I, too, could grow lithe as a red serpent,
so I, too, could swim in a sacred lake.

continued...

V.

I walked to Ráquira, traced the cracks in the cobblestone square—
its lightning trail led me to a shop
where an old man lathed hard nuts
until they were baskets, eggs,
or the smallest candle the length of a termite,
the smallest candle burning like the one
stationed within the body of Chiminanagua, who is
the creator of all things—the whole almond filled with clay.

VI.

I spoke to the chicle-man.
He had a street-stand,
a dirty chair on the corner.
He sold mango-on-a-stick.
He yelled—*Aftershocks!*

I turned to my left.
I stared at another man with dirty fingernails.
I saw his hand, an infant bird's beak.
Reaching up, he knew no change would come,
no change without more winding of the way around him,
without more chances for a passerby,
more chances to get away from his sitting,
his sitting against the cathedral wall,
more chances to escape the wanting,
the focusing on the opportunity to buy
a new *Daily Times*, hot coffee and milk,
no sugar.

The cardboard aura of this man
was pigeon droppings, was a shrine to simply take
what is given, to resolve the gift of its weight,
stake an exchange that tempers
that awareness of less,
that small peel of what was more fried fish.

Taking out my last coin,
(I didn't want to break a twenty),
I tossed a bit of metal.
I wondered: *Does his knee drag and burn?*
He heard, whispered: *What's left of this leg doesn't turn or stand.*
What's left of this leg is listless,
a large node on the end of my hip.

continued...

A propane gas truck roared the corner.
Shining the headlights at dusk, it caught orange dust in the beams.
The seeming-for-a-moment made the man concrete—a saint,
a saint who fell from the cathedral tower.

VII.

On the opposing side of the street, I met two men even older.
I met two men who'd hammered tin bowls into armor and helmets.
They'd cruised downtown to mock the morning traffic.
The tall one rode the mule.

I took their passing to be a sign to go
out into the countryside, to go watch my grandfather
shadow a snake-eating-a-rabbit on a whitewashed wall.

Later, the children slept to a tune his hands plucked.
He plucked a string on a stick.
In the morning, he strummed and hummed.
He sang, ¡Qué dolor!

Pulling potatoes from sloping fields,
he checked for disease. The yellow *papas* passed his tests.
He moved on to vaccinate pigs.
At 7:00 a.m., sleeves rolled above elbows,
he examined the pregnant cow,
her calf due this coming September.

He told me, *The gold in the valleys*
are tears of Bachúe, She with Large Breasts—
your grandmother—is memory, is obsidian
and tagua nuts, eyes of splintered lightning
mapping the savannahs.
He reminded me that I know
little can also hold much, armadillo blood for drinking—
the cure for asthma attacks on dusty roads.

continued...

VIII.

The following day I remember calling a drunk
madder fodder
for driving a motorcycle,
for knocking Grandfather to the ground,
for crushing his head.
It happened, and I am forever hanging
half a calabash below my breasts,
a bowl for sheltering my head
against rabid waterfalls,
a bowl for washing in saltier waters.

IX.

I pound sand with Grandfather's cane.
With each thud, I make thunder.
Whistling, wet fern, caught in the tread of my boots,
plants an archipelago, tracks a green path,
an island chain across the Panama Canal.
And I swear I'll pray,
until I die I'll pray—*Snake Shadow*.

The First Dance

Mother lay on her side, propped up on pillows,
her heart waving the stark room. The beat
captured a screen. Flawless, it relayed
the waxing moon.

I saw the source of first sound,
memory of life before *luz*. Waves
roused me to move,
mountain rhythms relaying
the waxing moon.

In a cumbia trance, I rocked,
safe in my mother's womb. While we danced,
my heart echoed her rhythm, relayed
the waxing moon.

Adolescent American

When Jimmy called me a spic,
his sister told. She told her dad
who stepped on Jimmy's back
while Jimmy did push-ups.

But what I remember now is Jimmy
doing push-ups. He was showing off,
not really caring about my heritage,
more the small breasts, and hips widening,
more my slow walk with his sister.

What he really wanted was to see
the fire light up in my brown eyes.

Periluna

Dreaming again, Tatiana followed the small moon in her mind.
She saw the tears of her mother pool in its craters,
saw them dry, saw the saline fade
the gray into the dusty white of ash.
Her mother mourned over an open gash, over the final burn
of a last chapter turning—
the final peel of her own old mother's spirit from her chest.

A semilunar cusp of the heart was exposed to light,
though the sun had just set,
had cast a long shadow,
had sheltered Tatiana's eyes,
waking her to the dark of a new moon.

El Motivo

Sergia weaves herself a ruana–
llama wool dyed red,a covering with a hole for the head,
another reminder to push through,
a reminder of Father's love for Mother,
her worth to protect,
so the head can clear the opening,
so the eyes won't lose the periphery,
so the corners can serve as a compass,
just as the four directions start the weave.

Grab a Stick

Quick, what will you beat out—
     the egg with yolk bleeding,
     the soul to her last pleading,
     or the cumacu rhythm my hips circle?
Will you knock the dust from the ruana?
Will you lift your ruana from your neck?
Will you let it become a part of the landscape,
let it be a prayer to rest on, a place to lie down,
a place to count the fires by the scent of smoke,
count them when the wind shifts?

When Magdalena Descended

Before she was a river, Magdalena was an unbroken wave,
gliding above time in the Caribbean. Tired of the endless coming,
never going, Magdalena asked a passing fish
where he got the body-ripple, the propulsion
of weight through water.

His answer: *I crossed the Atlantic,*
was pulled by a current.
The feel of it pounded my heart.
I let go, and it took my head
a little to the left, tail a little to the right,
until the center-body sprang forward,
until I was on my way to a coast
sanded with the sound of blood,
blood reverberating off the eardrums.

Heart on her tongue, Magdalena shouted to a bird:
Where'd you get the beat of your wings through air,
the tight swell of flight that wakes your feathers?
The bird in a burst of cosquillosa-laughter,
called on a wind from the east.
The wind dipped, snared Magdalena in a waterspout,
unhooked the locks in her spine.
Diving, she descended as a whip
down the diagonal length of her country.

Wet Claw, Half-Eaten

What the ear is accustomed to hearing,
what it rarely hears: a music of honey,
the certain placements of accent—wet claw, half-eaten.
The movement of the tongue
through the algae of an 'r'—the palm frond
drifting on an ocean of animal sorrow,
and the sound that smells of clean jars—the tired
call of a mother under blankets, feathers,
naming her desert Volcán of Wandering Roots.

Arracatacataca

Two natural parents, I've two naturalized parents,
Father from the North, Mother from the South.
The two, they dance.
They dance cumbias, waltzes around the living room.
Lots of dancing, dancing around a vacuum, dancing,
especially at the New Year, while I giggle,
wave one hand in the air, my hips following
the order of my mother's. They turn,
he spins out to sit, to watch her,
while Brother laughs, claps,
holds his children close.

Agua Panela

I.

Caliente, it's hot
water and sex.
Sugar, raw,
melted in a steel hand-bowl.

A whole block is broken.
The small, unequal pieces
are dropped through steam,
are dissolved.

What's seen is true:
a daughter learning
she has to light
the stove.

II.

A child's a truth-teller:
Papito, yesterday
me and Mami
went to the blue house again.

She was left. One ought not leave a child
playing in the center garden of the local house for lovers.

The walls and windows of every room exposed,
whether open or closed, a child
knows without knowing: *courtyard—*
the word for what remains of hard-memory.

continued...

III.

She adds cinnamon
so medicine for children
can taste as it should.

Like rice pudding,
a woman could forgive
her honesty as a child,
wrap herself in hand-woven wool
dyed orange, pink,
could sip something warm to relax
her heart muscle.

II.

Birthright

Mother, you turn mirrors during storms. You fear
the reflections, the call-down of a strike…

Eyes that have seen
something they never should have—
lightning, a swell passing over us.
I face history in your eyes, Mother.
At seventeen, I saw my birth certificate.
I wasn't recorded with the name you gave me.
Angry in a changing ignorance, I threw "why" like knives.
You caught them in your teeth, you explained:

> *Your middle name, Maria,*
> *is all yours, your grandmother's legacy.*
> *I had let yours go,*
> *just on paper—*Marie.
> *I thought—we had to*
> *be in English.*

I took our name back, Mama,
when I married, legally claimed what you call me,
what you have always called me,
who you have always been—
Mother in a Storm of Lightning.

La Despierta

Tatiana is dancing, naked under a black t-shirt.
She was painted onto a leaf, was painted to lock her in,
painted to cover up the veins, to hide what was once alive.

But she's flown off. She's revived and dancing,
her toes scuffling across a worn carpet,
her hips lost in the momentum of a drum,
toenails polished red,
arms open and reaching *la dicha*,
la dicha swelling in her chest—her joy unfolding her shoulders.

She won't stop this, won't lose the glory of her spine
vibrating the rest of her again,
vibrating like a bass string moving the air in rounded waves.

She wakes in the morning to hear a conga,
wakes to hear the cries of men calling out their songs,
wakes to shake off the sleep, to circle her pelvis to an old,
Caribbean beat,
a beat carried across an ocean,
a beat that's blessed her with the momentum of a drum,
a drum that shook her off a leaf, freed her,
restored her to nakedness under an old, cotton shirt.

La Costa

Riding the wave of your collarbone, my fingertips
trace your chest, trace the valley of your sternum.
Each spiral of my *huella*, my fingerprint,
trills a current up my wrist, arm,
a current across the shoulder, pouring into my chest,
pooling, caught in a freshwater cave,
the cave you bathe in,
the water you run across your face,
the water cleaning the salt from your reef-cut cheek.

Té de Límon

    —para Miguel

Papi, when you take out the knife,
pass the blade across the oiled flesh
of fresh límon,
your hand—the grace of one
well-placed beat—runs the steel down
to the rind, through the meat,
the juice brought to the edge of bursting
until you hold a half and squeeze,
wind with your warm, clean hands
and crush a world that fills the pan with the sour
jugo
de límon.

Heated with water and honey,
the rind remains—its oils
calm
the cough into quiet
sleep
where a man hums
lullabies,
holds a child in a tender dance,
cradles her above the kitchen floor
in his arms—a slow tide
she rides to the shore of ease,
free of the hagridden night.

Look Longer

Rain's coming, see the weave,
see it in the patterns of the hammock.
The Bright Star again. She's come again,
she and her interlocking triangles, two joined
end to end, two holding the secret of emeralds.
The rain coming, the rain held in two triangles,
the joining, the secret of emeralds,
many smaller, many held together by the two,
held together for later
when the rains come...

Menta Negra

My hair, the black mint you drink into your hands,
the black mint you gather and rub on my neck,
is the midnight intent you pulp, you tincture and run down your face,
the warm calm, the fragrance loosed to quiet the grief in your lungs,
the warm calm, the black mint, the midnight labiatae...

The Queen of Colombia

> *So [it shall be] that he who invokes a blessing on himself in the land*
> *shall do so by saying, May the God of truth*
> *and fidelity [the Amen] bless me...*
> Isaiah 65:16 Amplified

Juana de Santana changed her testimony.
She changed her testimony because she couldn't remember
the length of days.
She was lost in the awe of the Virgin's cheeks illuminating
on drab linen,
lost in awe when the Virgin walked off her painting,
alive, a woman not wanting to be set up so high,
a woman who wanted to sit in the pews, to gather
into the spice of prayer,
a woman who wanted to collect the hard seeds strung on her rosary,
slowly letting them fall through her fingers.
She wanted to plant them
knuckle deep in the earth of her breath.

Gracia's Walk

She crosses a four-lane road,
a load of laundry
and a baby
balanced on her hips.

In socks and sandals, she's ageless,
her hair magnificent, bound loosely
to free her eyes,
to not hinder her focus.

She has one room,
a bed,
and a stove
where she creates
life between arepas
and sheets. She feeds
her man
with hands that pat
and knead.

I'd like to be her walk,
to ask her
what a mother needs,
where her love bled
and how she healed him with aloe,
then agua, poquito salado.

Namesake

> *–for Aura*

Aura, not the mood but the name,
is my aunt washing on a concrete slab.
She's the one with the secret of bleach,
how to rid oneself of a stain.

From her, I learned to paint
fingernails, to turn down serenades,
not to be so easily flattered.
And then there's the walk,
the cool lift of her chin to look to the right or left.
She's the proper way to make rice—
not too much burning on the bottom of the pan,
just enough to savor the toasted grain.

We hand down, from niece to niece,
the black velvet shawl of first desire—its fall from a horse,
the toss into barbed wire,
a scar left on the calf, below the back of the knee.

When your name is sung for the first time,
the Maria in the middle becomes a chorus.
The women who've handed down, are mothers
are aunts singing like slick, wooden
stairs to slide down. The walk back up
puts the curve at the base of our spines.

When your name is sung for the first time,
the Maria in the middle knows a claim
will come through sex, will come,
will land in the guacharaca
rhythm of a woman's walk,
knows another woman will come,
will call back the victory of chronic revolutions.

Her Resurrection

Rocking in an orange hammock before sunrise,
the moon still bright, the bamboo blooming, Tatiana can consider
the beauty of lying above ground, in between trees,
the beauty of knowing the dead branches will hold,
because the roots run deep,
because the deep roots widened their girth, strengthened their grain.

One hand on a hip, preferring

the loose mouths of rivers,
the coupling of the semi-supernatural
gardenia to an ear.
I left the desert, had to find the burial urns
along the lower Magdalena,
had to touch the birds on the handles,
had to look, see their stare,
and pick out the bones of the armadillo they guard.
My fingers remembered the roll of them,
not to crack open to marrow,
but to seed them, they are
the holy seeds of pigweed.
I sowed the bones, waited for Chuchaviva,
the Rainbow—the Patron of Those with Fevers and
Women in Childbirth.
He's the sign, the covenant between Bochica and mankind.
Yes, he could be
the same you're thinking of, God
not being one to limit Himself
by place or name or language.
I waited for my fever to break.
I waited for my belly to swell and drop,
waited to have a child to take to Bucaramanga.

Numina

A brown velvet dress dips down her chest,
is worn to celebrate lines that bend and move away,
lines that expand laterally into sloped vistas.

A mother bent to lift a child that isn't her own,
but whom she bore so his head could rest on the yielding
inclination to forget himself.

Chispa en la Barriga de Dios

Crisp wind runs cold in bones at Friday's dawn
Sun rails higher, praise-lit to fire morning

Until marrow warms red the song the heart hums
And life again rejoices with fern

Bowed in prayer and wet with cloud forest dew that sweetens
The yellow clay we take into our hands

This child I hold leans his back against my squatted body
Anchored between my bent knees he hears
The flit and trill subtleties of the birds waking

He rolls the clay into balls, closes one in his fist and
Opens his palm to say,

Moon
Mama

I look down to small burrows of earth
Where our fingertips burnished

Bowls at our feet and remember the night he said
Bring down the moon
Please Mama

I told him her size and weight and length away
Until he reasoned *I fly*

I hold you
You no fall

And sister
No fall Mama

K?

La Virgen de Chinquinquirá

Isabel saw Mary, La Inmaculada,
leave the altar for arnica and aniseed.

Mary was longing for the simple—
cedar for the siding of her womb, its grain wooling,

warming the walls with a liberated light,
a light that arches into the arteries of the church ceiling,

arches into ardent, rising streams blushed with ground annatto.
Her cheeks, now anointed, are finally full with noon.

III.

A Killing in the State of Cauca

In Santander de Quilichao, Alvaro,
an indigenous priest, was ground and bled into mortar.
The mortar was spread over concrete block.

He preferred that his blood be mixed with clay,
that it be a living adobe,
a border between the family inside
and the war out.

He'd urged a stop to concrete,
was killed for suggesting bamboo—
free and flexible, the walls wouldn't crash,
wouldn't crumble in the frequent movements of earth.

The Sugar Beet Prayer

May taxes on rice and beans be abolished into the coal creases
of a condor's wing.
May mortgage payments fall like bread from a tenth-story window.
May the endless beatings end, may they be overcome
by the abundance of red corn
        packaged and hanging at the end of a grocery aisle.
May the machete-murder to steal a truck from an old man
        be purged by the consumption of the bloody seeds
of the tamarillo,
may it be redeemed of its fleshy binding in the mind.

Refining Sugar

Great Uncle Iván died in a vat,
boiled in cane juice on his family's farm.
Iván fell into the oversized, cast-iron kettle.
His brother had to kill him to save him,
had to shoot him before the skin finished blistering,
rising off his flesh, coated in unsulfured molasses.

His mother folded each moment into the turning of her mind.
His mother looked on, each bend of his arms, his legs…

As his body poured out, she held him to what she knew—
his smile, the dimple between his eyes when he cried,
and how, as boys, his younger brother had chased him,
tripped him so they rolled together like pups behind the hacienda,
here, she watched that same brother hold Iván's cooled body,
his skin glazed, only tufts of black hair left on his head.

Today, out of respect, we're careful not to sing sugar
or coo too sweetly to the children,
we tell them the truth—that it's hard on our family.
We tell them our bodies don't take it too well.

Peace Negotiations

Bodies, like subtitles
captured within the frame of a dream that won't wake,
women dead, bare-chested, thrown to the side of the road.

A child sees from the backseat: the swell of rotting stomach.

While in another room, a president and rebel leader
talk over gourmet potato salad and pita,
between them a common beer:
      worms in the intestines,
      parasites causing nightmares
and teeth-grinding.

Terremoto

The photo: hands clasped, hands surging out of concrete, iron rebar—
all that's left of an apartment building in Pereira.

Quicks burning, the fingernails burrowed the rubble
burrowed like digging sticks
moving earth aside, like digging sticks pushing through to sky...

The caption didn't mention: one hand was a man's
unearthed to hold a woman's.
Both buried, they'd found each other's fingers,
squeezed night through a last breath.

Cáscara de Coco

Tip the coconut
Crack it
Crack it

You need the shell, man
Crack the hard and hollow
Shell
Shatter it
She likes
Polished shards
Of the coco
Crack and
String pieces
Shards to hang
From her neck
A necklace of shards
Polished and strung
Shards she slides
Between her breasts
Slides across her chest

Crack it
Crack it
Make her something beautiful

The Suicide of El Dorado's Wife

I dove into Lake Guatavita, the Anxiety of Too Much Rain,
with a rosary of ironwood beads
carved with a good knife.

A blue tassel of yarn sprays from the bottom of the cross,
and as I count prayers,
weight lifts from my wrist.

But I'm still diving, ignoring everything.
I'm still digging into the basin, sifting with my fingers
for my daughter's eyes.
By now, they must have passed
through the Serpent of the Dead who ate them,
who reigns in the lake, who stole
her vision into the white paste of his bowels.

I hear the chanting of my husband. He thinks he can dissolve light
into the lake,
hopes his body coated with honey, dusted with gold,
will find us. But he won't see, he won't hear me choke
on the gold dust in my esophagus,
the gold dust churning my phlegm,
the honey binding me to grass roots,
tearing my rotting skin.

All he'll recover is the green body of my daughter's infant corpse,
all he'll have is her hollow stare.

Tia's Request

When the children's hands are burnt,
deep ocean clams, take a berry from a brittle bush.
Rub the juice into their knuckles,
and in the stained creases of their fingers,
you'll read their true names.

Teach each to spell with coarse charcoal, cooled,
carried from the fire lit for them to dance around
like a ring of stars, like a blaze of wind
twirling after a hailstorm.

They'll mark the stones that line the fire-pit.
They'll mark them with budding scratches, cups,
gateways for broken-water-trails,
arroyos crawling ahead, long stretch marks,
long stretch marks on a woman's thighs…

Tell the children not to damn the mists.
Before the sun sees another rising,
let them growl. Remind them to slide
their feet in the grass. Remind them to wax water
out of berries of ice. Remind them to celebrate when water comes,
to celebrate that it came again, loosening
a weight from the night air, from the heaviness of hands.

Ars Poetica

Dry heaving on my mother's bed,
I'm asked to stop. But I won't.
In a dream I'm told the slobber
drooling from my lips is *chala*.
When awake, I know the dryness
pouring from my abdomen
is corn husks.

Gathering them with the closing of my arms,
I carry the dry leaves outside to the irrigation well.
Within each veined paper leaf, I roll
the white pith of sunflower stalks.
I rub the inside of my hands with blackberries,
print my palm on the outside of each,
then drop one at a time, each message down
and wait...

A voice falling from the pine above asks, *Would you bathe in it?*

Knowing the answer, I dive,
wonder, *Which berry offered*
the most dye, which would bear a stench,
which a stain? Will the purple
marks on the main rib of a leaf
survive the trip down the ditch?

This being the mud in my bones,
I rest on river water—
a floating rib.

Twelve Poems for Mama, Her Hands, and the Fire They Started

I.

Roped-soled sandals and ruanas are worn by children
south of the equator. They eat ants, weave hammocks,
hope for pan de queso and cocoa.

The Duck, Nunuma, the upturn of her tail,
her tail like a bromeliad leaf, a striped tongue,
a striped tongue that speaks,
sings the light and dark green of feet meeting water.

II.

Gregorio points out a cedar tree,
a sleeping mirla—a dark bird.
All dark birds unbraided from their flock,
flying in six directions, know there are seven.

continued...

III.

Weaving sombreros at Sandona, Nariño,
Estera makes a point about dyeing with nogal—
American walnut, as you may know it.

Browning the fibers of iraca palm,
adding a whistle to a beat,
a beat that won't be ignored—the atriums wheeze,
the chest rumbles.

IV.

Only the hummingbird flies backward,
a blurred word parallel to Earth,
the first word just beyond comprehension,
the letters in a dream, a message
turned to ash in the memory,
though it burns in the blood.

continued...

V.

Hearts at rest beat a thousand times per minute,
and the hats from Sampúes can't keep up with that breeze—
they lift, land in banana trees, freeing the hair to a distant cloud.

Tomorrow rests on cotton squares
arranged and spattered with prayers—stones,
leaves, a hummingbird wing,
river water...dream.

VI.

The center of the crown is woven into a cross.
Estera, is she fond of you,
is she fond of your arrow cane hat from Sampúes,
the place of gourds, rattles
where Mother speaks for the dead,
uncles whose names she can't remember?

continued...

VII.

Iwouya, the Bright Star, announces the arrival of rains,
the arrival of elliptical stains that dye the dry clay.

Gregorio's middle and ring fingers reach out to spread
the culture of burnt banana leaf,
the smoke blackening the senses, the lungs of memory,

as a drop is smeared on the burning cheek of Earth,
Pachamama, the Crude Silver Ore crafted to keep the finery
fair, to keep the salt beds
salinized and rising.

VIII.

Bochica carved the patterns for crafting into the side
of the northern Andes,
into the Cordilleras. He carved them to remind
the descendants of the Chibcha to keep
their hands in earth, to remind them of the freedom
of a loose, woven shirt
lying on the floor, to remind them of a woman in a walnut chair,
her breasts for feeding, bare to nurse.

continued...

IX.

The locals warned, *Duida,*
Duida is occupied and dangerous.
Yet, they know there are places where Mother is still
rain and aching, where she carries on,
where she makes life in an earth-oven,
where she lets smoke bake black into the edges,
where she insists carbon fleece the walls of her bowls.

X.

Bochica, the gray-haired sage in a ruana,
taught us to mold mud into bowls,
taught us to work gold into nose-rings
and ceremonial hoes.

He sings the methods for making.
He sings them into our memory.
We call back in syllables
no longer owned by any language or name.

continued...

XI.

Cucarachero, the Eater of Roaches,
the little house wren country people so love,
the little house wren has a song like achiote seeds,
small and red, good dye for the bedspread,
a rough cover for a country bed—the history,
the history of a family born of Bochica's daughters
and grandfather pirate, Tatapirata
who raped our mothers, who called
his sons white, his daughters wise.

XII.

Anyán Tepui, a cloud forest halfway to Duida,
has eyes of a thousand varieties,
blinks its wings on the face of an ancient scene—quinoa
and corn in baskets.

Today, a place for children to play,
a place high away from the chase of armed men,
armed men taking eight and nine-year old recruits,
taking children to shoot or train—more
grain for the caskets.

Eduardo in June

The something beautiful about a vaquero in a gray suit,
a felt cowboy hat,
the orange slack of his eyes at sunrise on the way to a funeral,
a vaquero in the back of a pick-up.
What a ride, the wind to consider...

About the Author

Erica Maria Litz graduated with an MFA in Creative Writing from Arizona State University. She is an Adjunct English Faculty at Paradise Valley Community College, an Adult Education Specialist for SRP-MIC, and poetry mentor with PEN Prison Writing Mentorship Program. Of Colombian heritage, her poetry has been influenced by the culture and the musical roots of Latin America.

Erica Maria Litz
PO Box 7332
Tempe, Arizona 85281

lluvialand@hotmail.com

www.ingramcontent.com/pod-product-compliance
Lightning Source LLC
Chambersburg PA
CBHW071840290426
44109CB00017B/1880